This book is published by Pomerak Ventures Ltd, registered in England & Wales under the company number 15578139.

POMERAK
ventures

ISBN: 9781917706070

# Introduction

If you're new to this book series, the title will give you a clear idea of what to expect. However, if you've read my previous two books about obscure facts, you'll see that this book is larger than usual. Instead of writing 500 facts like before, I've reached a milestone and included a thousand facts.

The book is filled with fascinating facts about Swindon, Stinson Hunter, obscure towns, price fluctuations, rankings, and amphibians. These intriguing nuggets of information are sure to ignite conversations, even in the most mundane situations when words fail you.

I got the main ideas for this book from pub quizzes I attend on Mondays when I'm not working. I was influenced by Tom Scott, Austin

McConnell, QI, and my years playing trivia games like Who Wants To Be A Millionaire?

I am also very aware of facts that have now been outdated in the case of records. Take Fact 141 from the first book: "*In the U.S., the most popular month for mothers to give birth is August.*" September is now the most popular month for mothers to give birth in the U.S. instead of August.

When I published this fact in my first book of facts in 2023, I was basing it on the most recent information available at that time. Many statistics show that most births occur between July and October, with conception typically happening in December.

Sometimes I get things wrong because I don't research enough or the information changes. In my first book, I stated that a film's duration was 73 minutes. However, after checking IMDB, Cult

Critic, and Rotten Tomatoes, I discovered that it is actually 75 minutes.

I didn't use a wide range of sources, so the facts in the book are condensed for simplicity and enjoyment. If I included all the sources for each fact, the book would be longer and more wordy. I apologize for potentially dumbing down the content of this series of books. I also apologise for any incorrect or outdated facts. If you find more such facts, please get in touch as I would be happy to include your name to thank you for your efforts.

I wanted to include some facts in this book, but I can't because of bad data from a source. According to a 2023 Cosmetic World survey, 43% of men find blonde hair the most attractive, 36% prefer brunette, 16% like red, 5% prefer black, and 1% like grey. However, the numbers add up to 101 instead of 100. I contacted Cosmetic World, but gave up after waiting for a month with no reply after more than 2 months. The author of the article is Monika Petite. If you're reading this, please verify the numbers in the opinion polls next time.

I still can't thank everyone enough for buying these books in the series, especially the first book which gained so much traction in 2023. So if you're a first-timer or regular to this series, thank you for your support! Bring on the useless information!

# 1,000 Useless Facts That Nobody Wanted To Know

1. The study of shoes and footwear is known as "Calceology".

2. The only national flag to depict the Holy Bible is that of the Dominican Republic.

3. "La Bougie du Sapeur" is a French satirical newspaper that is only published every 4 years on the 29th February.

4. Trinitrotoluene is the full name of the explosive TNT.

5. A study by Guinness found that around 162,719 pints of Guinness get stuck in facial hair in the UK.

6. "Lunar Larry" was the original name of Buzz Lightyear.

**7.** On September 9, 2002, Bart Sibrel made a forceful attempt to compel Astronaut Buzz Aldrin to take an oath, with his hand on a Bible, affirming that he had indeed set foot on the Moon. Later on that day, Aldrin punched Sibrel in the jaw.

**8.** D & G are the only letters in Scrabble worth 2 points.

**9.** As of 2024, British citizens do not require a visa to visit Mozambique for tourism purposes.

**10.** Aural atresia is the name of the phenomenon where a baby is born without an ear canal.

**11.** Boys are more likely than girls to be diagnosed with ADHD.

**12.** 18/50 is the same as 36%.

**13.** The shortest possible checkmate in Chess is where black wins after just 2 moves.

14. A perfect number is any positive integer that's equal to the sum of its proper divisors.

15. The first 6 perfect numbers are 6, 28, 496, 8,128, 33,550,336, and 8,589,869,056.

16. A "lynchet" is a kind of earth terrace found on hillsides, especially near Iron Age forts and other earthworks. It is commonly found in Southern Britain.

17. "George Washington's Breakfast" is the name of a book published in 1969 by Jean Fritz.

18. A YouGov report from 2023 found that only 3% of Brits never use cash.

19. "Tharg the Mighty" is the fictional editor of the British Sci-Fi comic, 2000 AD.

**20.** The name of the title character in the book series "Where's Wally?" is named "Waldo" in the U.S. and Canada, "Willy" in Norway, "Hugo" in Sweden, and "Walter" in Germany.

**21.** Pharasmanes III reigned in Iberia (what is now modern day Georgia) for 50 years between 135-185 AD.

**22.** "Chakapuli" is a stew origining from Georgian cuisine consisting of lamb or veal, cherry plums, and tarragon.

**23.** Tarragona in Spain is twinned with the city of Pompeii in Italy.

**24.** When Mount Vesuvius erupted in 1944, no military deaths were recorded from the eruption but 26 civilians were killed.

25. In June 2024, the website Google was visited for an average of 10 minutes and 41 seconds, according to SimilarWeb.

26. The National Gallery of Victoria in the Southbank suburb of Melbourne is Australia's oldest art museum.

27. As of June 2024, the cost of renewing a U.S. Adult passport book is $130.

28. According to Paste Magazine in 2016, the best letter of the alphabet is "Z".

29. "Cavatappi" is a type of macaroni formed in the shape of a helix.

30. A psammophile is a plant or animal that prefers to live in sandy areas.

31. In the UK, ivory can only be legally donated to museums if they were made before the year 1900.

**32.** On the 29th May 1900, the capital city of Chad, now called N'Djamena was founded as Fort-Lamy by French forces.

**33.** The city centre of Khartoum in Sudan has streets that are roughly laid out in the shape of a Union Jack.

**34.** The flag of Portsmouth is based on the personal arms of William De Longchamp. He was the Lord Chancellor of England when King Richard I granted Portsmouth market town status.

**35.** Portsmouth became a city on April 21, 1926, which is also the birthdate of Queen Elizabeth II.

**36.** Diorite has a hardness rating between 6 and 7 on the Mohs scale.

**37.** The final portrait of Queen Elizabeth II to appear on Bank of England banknotes first appeared on the £5 note on the 7th June 1990.

**38.** Mike Taylor from Boston, Lincolnshire is a well-known name and world champion in Unicycling.

**39.** Stinson Hunter is a supporter of Celtic football club.

**40.** "Embracery" is defined as an act of corruptly influencing a juror. The last conviction for Embracery in the UK was in 1975 but was later overturned.

**41.** Beethoven initially dedicated his Symphony No. 3, also known as "Eroica," to Napoleon Bonaparte. However, he later withdrew this dedication when Napoleon declared himself the Emperor of France.

42. Napoleon Bonaparte's famous story of leading younger students to win a snowball fight against older students only surfaced after he became famous.

43. Pascal's wager is a philosophical argument by Blaise Pascal. It states that if God exists, a person gains eternal happiness, and if God doesn't exist, nothing is lost.

44.     A bridge of Renaissance style is depicted on 50 Euro banknotes.

45.     The most forged banknote in the UK is the £20 note.

46. The world's largest brick made of bricks is a structure that stands at 25 feet in Montgomery, Alabama.

47. 20398 is a ZIP code in the United States based within the Navy Yards of Washington, D.C.

**48.** Aerosol paints have a ball inside to shake the paint; it's called a "pea".

**49.** There are on average 7 peas in a regular pod.

**50.** Ed Westwick, an actor who starred in Gossip Girl and White Gold, was born on the 27th June 1987.

**51.** Times New Roman, a font or typeface designed by Stanley Morison and Victor Lardent was designed in 1932.

**52.** Linux Libertine is the font used in the Wikipedia logo.

**53.** Indian Queens and London Apprentice are village names in Cornwall, England, named after local inns.

**54.** As of June 2024, 27 U.S. States still sanction capital punishment.

55. As of June 2024, Billy Bailey, who died in 1996, is the most recent convict to be executed by hanging in the United States.

56. Bocioc M Limited is a registered company in England with the official company number 12345678.

57. According to a Cosmetic World survey in 2023, 38% of women said the most attractive hair colour is brunette, 36% for blonde, 18% for red, 5% for black, and 3% for grey.

58. A 2024 Google survey found that the most mispronounced brand name is Nike, and the correct pronunciation rhymes with the word "key."

**59.** Medical professionals who violate the Hippocratic oath may not face direct punishment, but it is often argued that unprofessional behaviour could be considered medical malpractice.

**60.** "Bookkeeper" is the only word in the English language that has 3 consecutive double letters, 2 O's, 2 K's, and 2 E's.

**61.** "Mississippi" does not have the same distinction as above, but it's close. The letter I is sandwiched in-between the 2 S's, 2 more S's, and the 2 P's.

**62.** "Monte Tesoro" is a summit in Lombardy, Italy. It has a shrine that honours Italian soldiers who died in battle. The location of the place is in the Bergamasque Prealps.

17

63. KZY FM, also known as KKZY, is a radio station based in Bemidji, Minnesota broadcasting on 95.5 MHz.

64. Peter Allen and Gwynne Evans were the last people executed in the UK on 13th August 1964.

65. In 1987, the Italian jewellery company Nomination introduced a new bracelet made of stainless steel links, which later became known as the Nomination bracelet or the "Italian charm bracelet".

66. "Bray" is the name of two villages near the international border of Botswana and South Africa. As of their respective 2011 census readings, Bray, South Africa has the higher population.

67. The plural of the word census is "censuses".

**68.** The collective noun for geese is called a "gaggle", however "flock" is also used.

**69.** The group name for geese flying together is "skein," but if they are in a V-formation, it can also be called a "wedge."

**70.** Joseph Haydn's Symphony No. 101 is popularly known as "The Clock" due to a ticking rhythm during the second movement.

**71.** The Julian Calendar was used in Greece for civil purposes until the 16th February 1923 O.S. (1st March 1923 N.S.).

72. In the Gregorian Calendar, there are rules for determining leap years. A leap year must be divisible by four, except for end of century years. However, years at the end of a century must be divisible by 400. For example, 1900 was not a leap year, but 2000 was.

73. The collective noun for pomegranates is known as a "bushel" or a "basket".

74. According to a YouGov poll during the 2nd quarter of 2024, the most popular football club was FC Barcelona.

75. In a 2023 poll by Yardbarker.com, it was found that New York Giants fans were considered to have the least intelligent fanbase in the NFL.

76. "America's Top Colleges" is an annual ranking of colleges and universities in the USA conducted by Forbes Magazine since 2008.

77. In the 2023 ranking of America's Top Colleges by Forbes Magazine, Princeton University came out on top.

78. The term "Ivy League" refers to 8 top American universities in the Northeastern US: Harvard, Yale, Brown, Princeton, University of Pennsylvania, Columbia, Cornell, and Dartmouth.

79. Cornell University is the only Ivy League institution that was founded after the American Revolutionary War.

80. Moné Hattori is a Japanese violinist. She won 1st prize in the 11th Lipinski & Wieniawski competition for young violinists.

**81.** Tonga and American Samoa have the highest obesity rates for women, while Nauru and American Samoa have the highest rates for men. The estimates were published by the Lancet in 2024.

**82.** In the same research, Madagascar has the lowest rate of obesity in men at only 15%.

**83.** In April 2022, 27% of Americans believed that the stars and planets can influence our lives through astrology.

**84.** In a 2019 survey, 61% of Americans "strongly disbelieve" that the moon landing was faked.

**85.** A New England Journal of Medicine article reported 1,207 Reye's Syndrome cases in the USA from December 1980 to November 1997.

**86.** The artichoke is a member of the Sunflower family.

**87.** In 2024, an Indian Premier League cricket match set a new record for the loudest noise in a cricket stadium, reaching 131 decibels when Ajinkya Rahane of the Chennai Super Kings was dismissed.

**88.** The "Wright Solar" is a single decker bus built between 2000 and 2011 in Ballymenna, Northern Ireland.

**89.** "Vernayaz MC" is a railway station in the Swiss canton of Valais.

**90.** The average person in the UK will eat 7,560 chocolate bars, 2,268 slices of chocolate cake, and 8,316 chocolate biscuits in their lifetime, according to the British Heart Foundation.

91. Peter Czerwinski set the world record for eating the most Ferrero Rocher chocolates in one minute. He ate nine chocolates on January 4, 2012.

92. The first fatality in a powered aircraft was on 17th September 1908, seriously injuring Orville Wright and killing U.S. Army Lt. Thomas E. Selfridge.

93. It is possible for people with photosensitive epilepsy to give themselves a seizure due to rapid blinking.

94. When driving on highways, Sweden uses white paint to denote the centre line.

95. When driving on highways, Norway uses yellow paint to denote the centre line.

**96.** When driving on highways, Australia uses both white and yellow paint to denote the centre line.

**97.** "Traducere" is the Romanian word for translation.

**98.** An 18-inch-bladed fan can use up to 110 watts of electricity per hour.

**99.** In the early 1980s, future British prime minister Keir Starmer was caught by French police for illegally selling ice creams.

**100.** The first patent for a banker's lamp was filed on May 11, 1909, by Harrison D. McFaddin.

**101.** The word "toast" comes from the Latin word "tostum" meaning to burn or scorch.

**102.** According to scientific research, the time it takes to cook a perfect slice of toast is 3 minutes and 36 seconds.

**103.** Sten Gustaf Thulin is credited with inventing the modern lightweight shopping bag.

**104.** In Doctor Who, The Gelth were a humanoid species who used to have bodies but lost them in the Time War and became gaseous beings instead.

**105.** In 2023, the most popular programming language in usage was JavaScript.

**106.** The oldest European herring gull lived to 49 years old.

**107.** In 2023, the most popular Halloween candy in the U.S. state of Wisconsin was Butterfinger.

**108.** Up until 2018, it was illegal to publish or sell comic books depicting crime in Canada.

**109.** The world record for the largest collection of Pokémon cards is 32,809 different cards, held by Jens Ishøy Prehn and Per Ishøy Nielsen.

**110.** Duelling is technically not illegal on Pitcairn Island.

**111.** The word 'tattoo' in the military comes from the Dutch phrase "doe den tap toe", meaning "turn off the taps". In the 17th century, this call was used to signal innkeepers to close and soldiers to return to the barracks. This has no relation to the origins of an ink tattoo.

**112.** The most popular ink tattoo design in the USA is a butterfly.

**113.** China produces nearly half of the world's cabbages, while Russia consumes the most cabbage per person.

**114.** Only Belarus and the United Kingdom use the first past the post voting system in Europe.

**115.** In the USA, the cheapest day to buy gas is usually Monday.

**116.** Most countries start the week on a Monday, but countries like India, Indonesia, Brazil, and the USA start the week on a Sunday, which is followed by most of the world's population.

**117.** Iran, Afghanistan, and Somalia are the only countries that officially start their calendar week on a Saturday.

**118.** Listerine, a popular mouthwash brand today, was originally made for surgical antiseptic and floor cleaning.

**119.** In a 2017 survey, the average British household owned 104 books, and statistically book ownership increases with age.

**120.** Avocados are not fruits, or vegetables; they are berries.

**121.** David M. Smith is credited as the inventor of the clothes peg.

**122.** The average cost of a funeral in the United Kingdom in the year 2023 was £3,953.

**123.** Dyrehavsbakken is the oldest operating theme park in Klampenborg, Denmark. It opened in 1583.

**124.** 49 multiplied by 25 is 1,225.

**125.** The 16th word in the 16th chapter of J.D. Salinger's "The Catcher in the Rye" is "Sally".

**126.** "Flugelbinder" is a made-up word from the film "Cocktail". It refers to the aglet or aiglet, which is the small tube at the ends of a shoelace.

**127.** Most carpets last anywhere between 5 and 15 years.

**128.** The Maldives is the country with the highest divorce rate.

**129.** In morse code, the letter 'T' is represented by a singular dash.

**130.** The Rotokas language spoken in Papua New Guinea is known for having the smallest modern alphabet, with only 12 letters.

**131.** The study of smells and odours is known as "aromachology".

**132.** Ireland has the highest rate of credit card fraud in Europe, with 88 out of 1,000 people being victims of this type of fraud.

**133.** A Cadbury Creme Egg contains 177 calories.

**134.** "Stamps!" was a 2023 collage artwork composed by Jack Soley that was sold at auction on the 8$^{th}$ November 2023 for £2.

**135.** Will Smith turned down the role of Neo in The Matrix, instead starring in the 1999 film, Wild Wild West.

**136.** Actor Tom Hardy released a rap mixtape in 1999 called "Falling On Your Arse in 1999" using the pseudonym 'Tommy No. 1'.

**137.** The name of a highly skilled roller of cigars is known as a "torcedor".

**138.** Male toads chirp to tell other males not to mate with them.

**139.** The Electra 279 tumble dryer was manufactured in the UK from around 1971 to 1975. Not much else is known about these machines, as not too many of them are still around.

**140.** Mattel says you can't stack draw cards in UNO. If the last card played is a draw or wild draw card, the next player has to draw the cards it says.

**141.** There is a Catholic version of UNO called "Unus Deus". The official Kickstarter campaign for the game says, "*Instead of random colors, it uses liturgical colors, and instead of meaningless numbers, it uses the symbols of our Faith.*"

**142.** The # symbol has many commonly used names such as hash, pound, number sign, hashtag, hex, octothorp, sharp, and square.

**143.** ASCII is an acronym which stands for the American Standard Code for Information Interchange.

**144.** Humans pass wind roughly between 13 and 21 times a day.

**145.** A 'zarf' is the name given to the usually metallic holder or sleeve of a coffee cup.

**146.** The modern cardboard coffee cup sleeve was invented in 1991.

**147.** Shizo Kanakuri holds the record for the longest time to finish a marathon. He started the race on July 14, 1912 and finished on March 20, 1967, a total of 54 years, 8 months, 6 days, 5 hours, and 32 minutes.

148.   A piece of music that's played "pianissimo" is played very softly.

149.   During the Great Potato Famine, schools in Ireland taught crochet to help people earn money to move to America, as many Irish made a living by selling their crochet creations.

150.   There is no official Himalayan Salt Lamp Day.

151.   The first Saturday in October is Global Cardboard Day.

152.   The world consumed approximately 414 metric tons of cardboard in the year 2022.

153.   Yum Yums are a sweet treat that originated in the Netherlands which consists of a twisted doughnut coated in icing.

**154.** During World War One, tanks had genders; male tanks would be armed with six-pound guns, whereas female tanks would only equip machine guns.

**155.** Alec Issigonis designed the Mini car, which was later recognized as the 2nd most influential car of the 20th century.

**156.** The winner of the most influential car of the 20th century, was the Ford Model T.

**157.** Bus drivers have the highest depression rate compared to other professionals, according to a study published in the journal of Social Psychiatry and Psychiatric Epistemology in 2014.

**158.** The English novelist and short story writer J. G. Ballard was born in Shanghai.

**159.** Most shoppers on the Temu app are aged between 25 and 34 years old.

**160.** In France, TGV stands for "Train à Grande Vitesse," which translates to "high-speed train" in English.

**161.** Coconut pearls are believed to be the rarest gemstones in the world. However, their existence is controversial, with some people claiming that published photos of these pearls are fake.

**162.** 42nd Street in Manhattan, New York is exactly 2 miles long.

**163.** Crystal Palace was a glass and cast-iron building originally built for the Great Exhibition of 1851. It was destroyed in a fire in 1936.

**164.** The tallest building in the world in the year 1500, was Lincoln Cathedral. It was the tallest building ever until the construction of Ulm Minster, in 1890.

**165.** The name Zinc is of unknown origin. It could possibly come from the Persian word "sing" meaning stone, or the German word "zinke" meaning spiked or pronged.

**166.** According to the Office of National Statistics, from 2001 to 2021, one person died in London due to exposure to air pollution, as recorded on the death certificate.

**167.** Trolling, casting, trapping, and handlining are all terms used in fishing.

**168.** In Greek mythology, Tyche was the goddess of chance; Fortuna was her Roman equivalent.

**169.** Arion was a fast, black-maned horse in Greek mythology. He is best known for saving the life of Adrastus, king of Argos.

**170.** The Argos Catalogue was a paperback released twice a year in British store branches. Each catalogue had over 1,600 pages with item descriptions, photos, prices, and catalogue/item numbers.

**171.** Salt and pepper shakers are among the most stolen items from restaurants in New York City.

**172.** There are 39 words in the first verse of Smash Mouth's 1999 single "All Star".

**173.** The ocarina is a wind instrument also known as the "potato flute".

**174.** "Ecumenical abuser" is a term coined by Judge Judith Sheindlin. It's about someone who makes fun of or mocks others they think deserve it, no matter their race, gender, or ethnicity.

**175.** "Irregardless" contains a double negative, but in common usage it's used as a synonym of "regardless." It first appeared in print in 1795.

**176.** Former UK Member of Parliament Justin Tomlinson made a bet with a Conservative MP at university that he would become Prime Minister by 2038. He stands to win £500,000 should this happen.

**177.** Yeovil Town's colours are green and white. This is referenced in their club anthem "Yeovil True".

**178.** Dermatillomania is a condition where people pick at their skin a lot, often due to stress, anxiety, or boredom.

**179.** The Pungsan Dog is a breed of hunting dog from Ryanggang-Do, North Korea. The dog is a rare breed and sometimes smuggled from North Korea to China. The Pungsan Dog is not a breed recognised by any major kennel club.

**180.**   Saint Eligius is famous for being the patron saint of horses. Additionally, he is also the patron saint of various professions, including goldsmiths, jewellers, coin collectors, metalworkers, veterinarians, and the Royal Electrical and Mechanical Engineers of the British Army.

**181.**   Cow Parsley and Giant Hogweed are similar plants, but giant hogweed has red spots on its stems while cow parsley does not.

**182.**   Shaving facial or body hair gives the hair a blunt tip, it might feel coarse  for a time as it grows out; but it does not change the thickness, colour, or rate of growth.

**183.** Coxinha is a popular Brazilian dish made of shredded chicken, dough, shaped like a teardrop, and deep-fried.

**184.** In São Paulo, "coxinhas" is also used as an insult for people with a boring lifestyle and conservative political views.

**185.** The Newman Arms in London, W1, is the pub that inspired the Proles Pub in George Orwell's novel 1984.

**186.** Thalassophobia is the fear of deep water.

**187.** The year 2024 is 2568 in the Buddhist calendar.

**188.** A pargeter is an alternative name for a plasterer.

**189.** A fluid ounce is equal to one-sixteenth of a U.S. pint and one-twentieth of an Imperial pint.

**190.** Wenceslao Moguel Herrera was a Mexican soldier who survived execution by firing squad after the Mexican Revolution.

**191.** The Coconut Monkeyrocket is the name of an electronic artist also known as Jason Emmett. His style of music that's "cartoony" and retro-sounding is self-referred to as 'electrokitsch' or 'toonbeat.'.

**192.** In July 2024, it cost 50 paises or 0.5 Rupees to send a postcard within India.

**193.** As of July 2024, the price to renew a driving licence in Ontario, Canada is $90 CAD.

**194.** It is illegal to name your baby "Spinach" in Australia.

**195.** The 'East Anglian Derby' is the name given to football matches between Norwich City and Ipswich Town. As of August 2024, Norwich has won the most games against Ipswich.

**196.** Scholars have tracked the first usage of the term 'transgender' to the 1960s.

**197.** According to the British Beekeepers Association, a beehive can produce 60 lbs of honey in a good season.

**198.** The Sarens SGC 250 is the largest crane in the world. It has a maximum lifting potential of 5,000 tonnes.

**199.** A ton is equivalent to 2,000 lbs in the Imperial system, while a tonne is equal to 1,000 kg in the metric system (around 2,200 lbs).

**200.** The world's oldest recorded joke was about farts and can be traced back to 1,900 BCE.

**201.** The most popular emoji used in Poland is the skull.

**202.** The most popular emoji used in Andorra is the Andorran flag.

**203.** The flags of Switzerland and the Vatican City are the only ones in the world that are square.

**204.** The 1928 Grand National set the record for the fewest finishers left in the race, with only 2 horses crossing the finish line.

**205.** In the Grand National horse race, there are 16 fences on the track, 14 of which are jumped twice. The largest of these fences is called "The Chair" measuring at 5 feet and 2 inches.

**206.** The first Drive-Thru wedding venue in the world is located in Las Vegas, Nevada. Bruce Willis and Demi Moore got married there.

**207.** The body of Charlie Chaplin was stolen from his grave in 1978.

**208.** George Mallory's fate remained a mystery until a research expedition found his body on May 1, 1999. Whether Mallory reached the summit before his death is unknown.

**209.** Belgium is the world's largest producer of billiard balls.

**210.** Only four countries produce hockey pucks: the Czech Republic, Slovakia, Canada, and the People's Republic of China.

**211.** Illusory superiority is a cognitive bias where people think they are better than others.

**212.** An excellent illustration of illusory superiority emerges from a study conducted in 1986, wherein a staggering 80% of participants expressed their conviction in being superior drivers compared to the average person.

**213.** Most of the world's unicycles are made in Taiwan.

**214.** As of 13$^{th}$ July 2024, there exist 1,672 editions of the Monopoly board game.

**215.** In 2024, Japan scrapped more than 1,000 regulations that required the use of floppy disks to submit government information.

**216.** The 1949 film, "Passport to Pimlico" is based on an original plot by T. E. B. Clarke.

**217.** The most common cause of car fires is a leaking fuel system.

**218.** The Grandmaster Chime Ref. 6300A-010 holds the record for being the most expensive watch ever sold at auction, fetching an astounding $31 million USD.

**219.** According to a 2021 survey by Hammonds Furniture, the least favourite household chore is ironing, followed by cleaning the oven.

**220.** In the same survey, the favourite household chore is vacuuming floors, followed by laundry.

**221.** The standard dimensions of a business card are 85 mm x 55 mm.

**222.** The 'Zeitpyramide' or time pyramid is a public artwork in Germany that has been under construction since 1993. A new block will be added once every 10 years and is scheduled to finish in the year 3,183.

**223.** The most common sleeping position is on the side.

**224.** The least common sleeping position is on the stomach.

**225.** Neptune is the only planet in the solar system not visible to the naked eye.

**226.** The Whiteley test is a medical questionnaire which checks levels of health anxiety or hypochondriasis.

**227.** Kamadeva is the Hindu god of love, desire, pleasure, and beauty.

**228.** "The Pleasure Song" is the 2$^{nd}$ song on Marianne Faithfull's 2002 album "Kissin' Time".

**229.** The unit for magnetic flux density is the Tesla.

**230.** From February 2023 to February 2024, the most common reason that Teslas failed their annual vehicle inspection (or MOT) in the UK, was due to defective tyres.

**231.** Brian Jackson is a British actor who was famous for his portrayal in the "Man from Del Monte" adverts from 1985 to 1991.

**232.** 245+183=428.

**233.** Using the pound coin, 50p, 20p, 10p, 5p, 2p, and 1p coins; there are 4,563 ways to make change for £1.

**234.** If the band Nine Inch Nails went metric, they would be known as the "22.86 centimetre nails".

**235.** Christo, born Hristo Yavashev, was a famous artist who gained international recognition for his unique use of fabric wrapping techniques in his art.

**236.** According to Wikipedia, "Uncyclopedia" is an encyclopedia filled with false information and lies, but one of the few accurate pages on their website is the 'About Uncyclopedia' page.

**237.** Akiko Yazawa was the world Backgammon champion in 2014 and 2018.

**238.** Your parent's sibling's grandchild is your first cousin once removed. And you are their first cousin once removed as well.

**239.**   It takes the planet Saturn 10.7 hours to make a full rotation on its axis.

**240.**   It takes the Moon around 27 days to make a full rotation on its axis.

**241.**   Cosmonaut Vladimir Komarov became the first fatality in spaceflight when Soyuz 1 crashed down to earth on 24 April 1967.

**242.**   3 days later, the now King Willem-Alexander of the Netherlands was born.

**243.**   A "rhyming reduplication" is a phrase where a word rhymes with a small change when repeated, usually using a different consonant. Examples include artsy-fartsy, easy-peasy, or willy-nilly.

**244.** "Razzle Dazzle" is a song in the musical Chicago. Its lyrics teach Roxie Hart how to lie in court, using a circus-like performance.

**245.** "Namby Pamby" is a minor character who stars in the 1991 film Drop Dead Fred, played by Elizabeth Gray.

**246.** "Boogie Woogie" is frequently referenced in Madonna's single "Music."

**247.** A person who plays a hurdy-gurdy is called a "hurdy-gurdist" or, if you're French, a "viellist".

**248.** "Hocus Pocus Junior: The Anatomie of Legerdemain" is a 52-page book first published by an anonymous author in 1634.

**249.** The world's biggest user and purchaser of fax machines is the UK's National Health Service.

**250.** A "pluviophile" is someone who finds joy and peace with rainfall.

**251.** In American English, a flashlight is called a torch in British English.

**252.** In American English, suspenders are called braces in British English.

**253.** "No Es Serio Tu Amor" is a song by Bruno Lomas first released in 1968. The song shares the same melody as The Supremes hit "You Can't Hurry Love".

**254.** According to a 1910 law still technically on the books in France, it is illegal to kiss on train platforms.

**255.** Vehicles in Saudi Arabia drive on the right side of the road.

**256.** All the UN member countries that begin with the letters H and V drive on the right side of the road.

**257.** The average professional worker receives 121 e-mails per day.

**258.** In Saudi Arabia, on December 3, 2020, the Aleradah Organization for Talented People with Disability broke the world record for the most text messages received in one hour. They received 19,649 messages.

**259.** Nostalgia was classified as a medical condition until the 20<sup>th</sup> century.

**260.** The first flavour of Doritos was toasted corn.

**261.** Since 2016, the roads within the city of Paris have no stop signs.

**262.**    Only the People's Republic of China and Vietnam impose the death penalty for fraud.

**263.**    Electrons have very little mass, so all the electricity powering the internet weighs about the same as an apricot.

**264.**    The very first web page went live on 6$^{th}$ August 1991.

**265.**    If you're born on the 6$^{th}$ August, you have the star sign Leo.

**266.**    Scientists have determined it would take 19 minutes to fall from the North Pole to the centre of the earth.

**267.**    The Alto Sanctuary released the ambient music album "Tranquil Voyages for Vivid Drifters" on September 1, 2023. The album is 34 minutes long.

**268.** Gampy was a character mentioned in The Legend of Zelda: Majora's Mask, He was Granny's late husband and the father of Tortus.

**269.** The international calling code for the Comoros is +269.

**270.** 270 in Roman numerals is CCLXX.

**271.** #FFC66E is the hex code for the Pantone colour Pale Marigold.

**272.** The most cited excuse for drivers caught speeding is that they didn't know the speed limit.

**273.** An average 1 kilo bag of rice can contain anywhere between 40,000 and 50,000 individual grains of rice.

**274.** As of the 13th July 2024, 52 grams of gold had a market price of 604,136 Japanese Yen.

**275.** In the TV series Columbo, his first name is never revealed; however, in 2 episodes where he shows his ID, his ID badge states his first name is Frank.

**276.** Adolf Hitler was nominated for the Nobel Peace Prize in 1939.

**277.** The collective noun for ravens is a "conspiracy" or an "unkindness".

**278.** The average age of a first-time millionaire is 37.

**279.** The old red telephone boxes in Britain were supposed to be green and silver, but that idea was abandoned because it would be dangerous for drivers.

**280.** The name for the Custard Cream comes from the Danish phrase "sensual treat".

**281.** By runs, the greatest win margin in cricket goes to when England beat Australia in the 1928-29 season by 675 runs.

**282.** Theoretically, the fewest numbers called for a full house in 90-ball Bingo can be as low as 15.

**283.** In many countries, a utility knife is commonly known by its trademarked name; "Stanley knife".

**284.** Berzins/Berzina is the most common surname in Latvia.

**285.** In 1745, Ben Franklin wrote a letter to a friend entitled "Advice to a Friend on Choosing a Mistress". In the letter, Franklin gives eight reasons why an older mistress is to be preferred.

**286.** In 1970, Cancún, Mexico, only had three residents. By 2020, the population was nearly one million.

**287.** In his later years, actor Marlon Brando spent a lot of time in AOL chat rooms, arguing about politics with strangers and often getting banned for using bad language.

**288.** Elon Musk's friendship with Google founder Larry Page ended over a disagreement about artificial intelligence.

**289.** The United States has more psychology majors graduating from college each year than there are licensed psychologists.

**290.** The Kingdom of Bhutan has diplomatic relations with only 54 other countries. Andorra, Luxembourg, Mauritius, Eswatini, and Fiji are among the 54. The United States, People's Republic of China, United Kingdom, Russia, and France are not.

**291.** From 1957 to 1976, there was a direct bus service from London, UK to Calcutta, India; the route took around 50 days to finish and cost £85 in 1957, which is around £1,726 in 2024.

**292.** King Abdullah II of Jordan can trace his ancestry back all the way to the prophet Muhammad.

**293.** Maine is the U.S. state closest to Africa.

**294.** The English Channel is known in French as La Manche, meaning "The Sleeve".

**295.** Velociraptors had feathers.

**296.** The Sahara has historically alternated between grassland and desert on a 41,000-year cycle. Barring human-driven climate change, it is expected to become green again in around 15,000 years.

**297.** In Vietnam, the Vietnam War is known as the American War.

**298.** Only about 3% of the soldiers who died in the Vietnam War were American.

**299.** The 20$^{th}$ digit of pi is 4.

**300.** The 23 enigma is a belief in the significance of the number 23.

**301.** Some fishermen believe that it is bad luck to have bananas on a boat because they think it prevents them from catching fish.

**302.** In June 2024, the global survey revealed that India's leader, Narendra Modi, had the highest approval rating of 70%.

**303.** The Gambia and The Bahamas are the only 2 countries with the word "The" in their name.

**304.** The first twenty minutes of the 1996 film Trainspotting had to be re-dubbed when shown in the U.S. Because audiences had a hard time understanding the Scottish accents.

**305.** According to a survey by Enjoy Travel, the Kiwi accent is the sexiest.

**306.** In the same survey, the Australian accent was 5th.

**307.** In 2024, a survey found that people in the South West of England were the most trusting of their neighbours compared to those in other parts of England.

**308.** A pun or a play on words is known as a "paronomasia".

**309.** The average age a person graduates in France is 24.1 years.

**310.** Queen Victoria of England was able to converse in Urdu.

**311.** In 2000, Jacob was the most popular baby name for boys born in the U.S., and Emily was the most popular for girls.

**312.** The most popular baby names in the U.S. In 2005, were Aidan for boys and Emma for girls.

**313.** British bathroom fixture manufacturer Armitage Shanks has its headquarters in Stoke-on-Trent.

**314.** The term "jibber-jabber" was first seen in the 16th century for the respective words to speak incoherently and rapidly.

**315.** Most homes in Paraguay don't have doorbells, and visitors instead clap their hands to announce themselves. This is considered more polite than knocking.

**316.**  The River Komoé in Côte D'Ivoire and Burkina Faso is 759 kilometres long.

**317.**  The name of an organism that lives and thrives in running water is a Rheophile.

**318.**  The name of an organism that lives and thrives in ants' nests is called a Myrmecophile.

**319.**  Someone who is passionate and has an interest in wine is called an Oenophile.

**320.**  A sommelier is a trained professional who has knowledge of many wines and is usually paid for their work, unlike oenophiles.

**321.**  Scotland is the world's largest producer of whisky.

**322.**  "Whisky" is from Scotland, Canada, and Japan, while "whiskey" is from Ireland and the United States.

**323.** The general rate of value added tax in Kenya is 16%.

**324.** In folklore, seeing a single crow can mean bad luck whereas seeing 2 crows signifies good luck.

**325.** ABBA's song "Waterloo" was banned on the BBC during the First Gulf War.

**326.** Vincent van Gogh sold only one painting during his lifetime. It was called "The Red Vineyard" and was bought by Anna Boch for 400 Belgian Francs, which is equivalent to £1,725.30 GBP in July 2024.

**327.** "I wanna run against the world that's turnin' I'd move so fast that I'd outpace the dawn, I wanna be gone; I wanna run so far, I'd beat the mornin' Before the dawn has come, I'd block the sun, If you want it done." is the chorus to the Hozier song De Selby (Part 2).

**328.** In a 2021 survey by Ipsos, the most trusted people were doctors, scientists, and teachers.

**329.** In the same survey, the least trusted people were politicians, government ministers, and advertising executives.

**330.** Restaurants in Montevideo, Uruguay banned table salt and condiments to address the country's obesity and high blood pressure problems.

**331.** In a 2024 survey, American voters decided that Joe Biden is more honest, yet Donald Trump was more mentally sharp.

**332.** The average IQ in Sweden is 97.

**333.** The global average age of menopause is 51.

**334.** The Hanuman Chalisa is a Hindu hymn that praises the deity Hanuman and is recited daily by millions of Hindus.

**335.** "Can Queen Victoria eat cold apple pie?" is a famous mnemonic that was used to teach the 7 hills that Rome stood: Capitoline, Quirinal, Viminal, Esquiline, Caelian, Aventine, and Palatine.

**336.** The smallest hill of the 7 hills of Rome is Viminal.

**337.** San Marino is the world's oldest republic. Its constitution dates back to 1600 and it wasn't admitted to the United Nations until 1992.

**338.** Harvey Hubbell is credited with inventing the household plug in 1904.

**339.** The British/Irish plug socket or Type G is widely regarded as the safest in the world.

**340.** NTSC and PAL are colour encoding systems widely used in television. NTSC delivers a frame rate of just under 30 fps and PAL delivers a frame rate of 25 fps.

**341.** Malta's largest export is refined petroleum.

**342.** In 2017, the UK's most popular pizza topping according to Papa John's was Mushrooms.

**343.** Chocolate truffles are named the mushrooms of a similar name because of their resemblance to the dark fungus.

**344.** The Piedmont white truffle or the Alba truffle is regarded as a prized truffle found in Italy.

**345.** White truffles tend to be more expensive and rare than black truffles.

**346.** The minimum driving age in the Maldives is 18.

**347.** Saint Lucia is the only country in the world named after a human woman.

**348.** "Brasil" is a mysterious island in Irish folklore. It is shrouded in mist except for one day every seven years. It appeared on maps as far back as the 14th century, but it has no connection to the present-day country with the same name.

**349.** The Fiat Strada was the most popular car in Brazil in the year 2022.

**350.** "Lackaday" is an archaic term for an expression of regret or sorrow.

**351.** Another archaic term for regret or sorrow is "Ruth".

**352.** All the pyramids in Giza have been looted.

**353.** Redruth, Cornwall is twinned with Mineral Point, Wisconsin.

**354.** The eighth commandment as mentioned in Exodus Chapter 20, verse 15 of the King James Bible is: "thou shalt not steal.".

**355.** The most stolen book in the world, is the Holy Bible.

**356.** According to a 2005 survey by Ipsos, cruelty is considered the biggest sin in the United Kingdom, even though it is not one of the "Seven Deadly Sins".

**357.** "Twelve Deadly Cyns...and Then Some" is a compilation album released in 1994 by Cyndi Lauper.

**358.** Nicole Kidman is a natural redhead.

**359.** The video game "Red Dead Redemption" is set in the year 1911.

**360.** Tadeusz Pietrzykowski was a Polish boxer who fought for the Polish Armed Forces and was held prisoner in Auschwitz-Birkenau and Neuengamme concentration camps during World War 2.

**361.** Fresh hay should make up around 80% of a rabbit's diet.

**362.** Cats are more popular household pets than dogs in Japan.

**363.** 1,052 people were killed in motor accidents due to a drunk driver in 2019 in France.

**364.** The cube root of 8,000 is 20.

**365.** In Olympic freestyle wrestling, there are 2 periods that are 3 minutes each with a 30-second break.

**366.**   The highest score in the Rugby World Cup was recorded in 1995. New Zealand won with a score of 145–17 against Japan. Despite this phenomenal achievement, New Zealand went on to finish as runners-up to South Africa in the tournament.

**367.**   In musical notation, Americans call it a "half note" whereas Brits call it a "minim".

**368.**   In the UK parliamentary general election of 2019, there were 164 reported cases of electoral fraud.

**369.**   More than half of your bones are in your hands and feet.

**370.**   A human will grow on average 600 miles of hair in their lifetime.

**371.** The production of tears will decrease with age, and a person will produce between 100 and 200 pints of tears a year.

**372.** Wanda is a female first name of Polish origin.

**373.** Sesame Street character Elmo is the only non-human to testify before the U.S. congress.

**374.** Elmo's birthday is February 3rd.

**375.** Sesame Street character Big Bird is 8 feet and 2 inches tall.

**376.** Big Bird's birthday is on March 20th.

**377.** In the French adaptation of Sesame Street, characters Bert and Ernie are respectively known as Bart and Ernest.

**378.** "The way to make people trust-worthy is to trust them." is a quote attributed to Ernest Hemingway.

**379.** There is no official national motto of Croatia.

**380.** The most stolen item in the East London borough of Tower Hamlets is Calpol.

**381.** The Calpol brand name comes from a contraction of Calmic and Paracetamol.

**382.** A stet is a term used in proofreading and comes from the Latin for "let it stand".

**383.** There are 4 calories in a Jelly Belly jelly bean.

**384.** If you lick 1,000 envelopes, you will consume 100 calories.

**385.** It's always better to mow grass before rain.

**386.** Cowboys believe that putting a cowboy hat on a bed will bring bad luck.

**387.** Butterfly eggs take around 3 days to hatch.

**388.** Watermelons are approximately 92% water.

**389.** The United States of America is the world's largest producer of blueberries.

**390.** Chia seeds were reportedly eaten by Aztec warriors to give them high energy and endurance.

**391.** 'Hinduism' scores 14 points in Scrabble.

**392.** 'Schadenfreude' in English Scrabble is worth 23 points, but in German Scrabble it's only worth 20 points.

**393.** In the year 1600, only 10% of women could read in England.

**394.** In the year 1900, New Zealand had the highest GDP per capita of $4,320 USD which is roughly $161,575 in 2024.

**395.** Haverfordwest is the county town of the Welsh county of Pembrokeshire.

**396.** Lemon juice is an ingredient in Hollandaise sauce.

**397.** "Here we are now, entertain us" is a lyric from Nirvana's 'Smells Like Teen Spirit'.

**398.** Facebook first allowed users to react to posts in 2016.

**399.** A cockerel features on the crest of Tottenham Hotspur football club.

**400.** Anne is the member of Enid Blyton's Famous Five that is first alphabetically.

**401.** Queen Anne of England was pregnant 18 times.

**402.** Shuttlecocks used in badminton weigh around 5 grams.

**403.** John Taylor of the USA was the first African American to win an Olympic gold medal.

**404.** In modern times, the first name 'Karen' has a negative stereotype of an entitled, privileged, and middle-aged white woman.

**405.** According to a study by Trustpilot, people named John and Lisa are most likely to leave one-star reviews.

**406.** A tenth of electricity generated in the U.S. comes from wind.

**407.** Outside North America, the store TJ Maxx is called TK Maxx to prevent confusion with British retailer T.J. Hughes.

**408.** Mark Everett is the lead singer of American band Eels; he was formerly known by his pseudonym "E".

**409.** Mark Everett released 2 rock albums under his E pseudonym, but they weren't released in the UK because the cover art had a big E on it, and he thought people might get confused.

**410.** Japan's national anthem is the shortest in the world with only 4 lines.

**411.** The collective noun for unicorns is a "blessing".

**412.** In architecture, a gargoyle is a decorative waterspout that directs rainwater away from a building's walls. On the other hand, a grotesque is a decorative carving that serves no practical function.

**413.** There are only 2 countries that contain the letter 'x' in their names, Mexico and Luxembourg.

**414.** Since 2020, all modes of public transport in Luxembourg are free of charge.

**415.** 92% of roads in Libya are paved.

**416.** Camels cannot swim.

**417.** Penguins cannot walk backwards.

**418.** A standard piano accordion has 41 keys.

**419.** Only 40% of people in Papua New Guinea have access to clean drinking water.

**420.** At current rates of production, the world's supply of oil will run out in 53 years.

**421.** A tarot deck has 78 cards: 22 major Arcana cards for spiritual lessons and 56 minor Arcana cards for daily experiences.

**422.** 43 x 61 = 2,623

**423.** Anne Lilia Berge Strand, professionally known as "Annie", is a Norwegian singer, songwriter, and DJ.

**424.** Aileen Quinn, best known for playing Annie in the 1982 film, received an honorary doctorate from Monmouth College in 2009.

**425.** Only 7 countries produce over 50% of the world's pornographic material. In decreasing order, these countries are the United States of America, the United Kingdom, Germany, Brazil, France, Russia, and Canada.

**426.** The 101$^{st}$ amendment to the constitution of India introduced a national goods and services tax from 2017.

**427.** Wyndham Halswelle won gold in the 1908 Olympics. He is the only athlete to win an Olympic title by default because his competitors were disqualified or withdrew.

**428.**   Macanese people are an ethnic group consisting of people mixed with mostly Cantonese and Portuguese ancestry. As of 2017, there are more Macanese living outside of Macau than within Macau.

**429.**   In English law, if 2 people die at the same time and the order of death of two persons is uncertain, the elder of the two is deemed to have died first.

**430.**   According to a 2024 poll by the Daily Mail, the pink wafer is Britain's most hated biscuit.

**431.**   King James I of England was also King James VI of Scotland.

**432.**   King James I of England was known as the "wisest fool in Christendom".

**433.** Pneumonia becomes double pneumonia when both lungs are affected.

**434.** Wernicke-Korsakoff syndrome is an unusual type of memory disorder due to a lack of vitamin B1 requiring immediate treatment.

**435.** Vitamin B1 is also known as thiamin.

**436.** The theremin is the only musical instrument you can play without making physical contact.

**437.** Rabbits are unable to vomit.

**438.** Contrary to popular myth, some goldfish have been observed to have memories that span for at least a month.

**439.** Oberon is a moon of Uranus.

**440.** Gucci is the most counterfeited luxury brand in the world.

**441.** The most popular surname in the world is Wang.

**442.** Psychologist Ty Tashiro says that around 15% of people struggle with social skills and communication, making them socially awkward.

**443.** The entire land area of the Philippines is as large as Olympus Mons on Mars.

**444.** ICAO airport codes are four-letter codes used to identify aerodromes worldwide. They should not be confused with IATA airport codes, which consist of three letters and are mainly used for luggage.

**445.** The ICAO has designed Jezero Crater on Mars, the code JZRO.

**446.** Imam Khomeini International Airport in Tehran was opened on 30th April 2005.

**447.** "Slapstick" is an American punk rock band from Elgin, IL with Brendan Kelly as main vocalist.

**448.** The Baader-Meinhof phenomenon, also known as frequency illusion, is when something you recently learned about suddenly seems to appear everywhere.

**449.** "Aserejé" is a made-up word inspired by The Sugarhill Gang's song "Rapper's Delight." It is a key part of the "The Ketchup Song" by the Spanish girl group Las Ketchup.

**450.** A 20.4 mm internal diameter ring is known as size V in the UK and size 11 in the USA & Canada.

**451.** Rival fans of the English football clubs Portsmouth and Southampton call one another "scummers" and "skates" respectively.

**452.** Radio DJ Mark Goodier was born in modern-day Zimbabwe.

**453.** Richard Sanborn, BA, MA, JD, coined imaginative collective nouns for hunters. He assigned the term "boast" to groups of successful hunters, and the term "grumble" to groups of unsuccessful hunters.

**454.** There are many collective nouns for librarians, such as cardigan, catalog, reference, shelf, shush, stack, volume, and whisper.

**455.**   Ramadan in the year 2025 will start on the 28$^{th}$ February and will end on the 30$^{th}$ March.

**456.**   Jrue Holiday is a basketball player who shoots jump shots with his right hand but prefers his left hand for finishing shots.

**457.**   British Prime Minister Lord John Russell claims that he had a private meeting with Napoleon on Christmas Eve in 1814. During the meeting, Napoleon remained silent and relieved himself in the corner of the room.

**458.**   Ciabatta is Italian bread invented by Arnaldo Cavallari in 1982.

**459.**   Nigel Mackenzie and Ian Dowding are credited as the inventors of the Banoffee pie. The dish was first devised in 1971 at the Hungry Monk pub, East Sussex, England.

**460.**   Historical records state that the Tiramisu dessert originated in Treviso in the 19th century, but some sources claim that the modern dish wasn't invented until as late as the 1970s.

**461.**   According to Strawpoll in July 2024, the 5 most popular German dishes in descending order are as follows: Schnitzel, Sauerkraut, Currywurst, Rouladen, and Bratwurst.

**462.**   Italian cuisine is the top-ranked out of the 100 best cuisines worldwide, followed by Japanese cuisine at number two and Greek cuisine at number three, according to Tasteatlas.

**463.**   A personal favourite from the same survey, Georgian cuisine was ranked 26th.

**464.** The first National Lottery draw in the UK took place on the 19<sup>th</sup> November 1994, the first number drawn was 30.

**465.** The majority of Americans disagree with the statement that hot-dogs are sandwiches.

**466.** "Crapmedia" is an anagram of Paramedic.

**467.** Pantone 13-1023 Peach Fuzz was chosen as the 2024 colour of the year by Pantone.

**468.** Juancho E. Yrausquin Airport on Saba, a small island in the Dutch Caribbean, has the shortest runway that is used by commercial aeroplanes.

**469.** Around 12% of people dream in black and white.

**470.** Before colour television was invented, only about 15% had dreams in colour.

**471.** Cambodia was the last country to get colour television, in 1986.

**472.** In the U.S., the most watched broadcast that wasn't a Super Bowl was the final episode of M*A*S*H in 1983. It had around 106 million viewers.

**473.** Pigs cannot look up straight up towards the sky.

**474.** Le Violon d'Ingres by Man Ray is the world's most expensive photograph, sold for $12.4 million USD at auction in May 2022.

**475.** As of 2019, a kilogram of Neodymium costs around $57 USD.

**476.** The world's largest moth is the Hercules moth from Queensland, Australia.

**477.** Humans are capable of recognising around 1 trillion different scents.

**478.** Reflexology is said to have originated in Egypt around 2,330 BC.

**479.** In Colombia, the practical driving test is scored out of 10, and you only need to score 5 to pass.

**480.** Driving licences issued in Argentina are blue.

**481.** Moroccan passports are green.

**482.** The eye colour of a baby can change between 3-6 months.

**483.** In cruise ship terms, MS means "motor ship" and MV means "motor vessel", these terms are used interchangeably.

**484.** Sam Denby is an American YouTuber known for creating several channels, including Wendover Productions, Half as Interesting, and Extremities.

**485.** If you set up an account on MySpace from 2003 until 2010, Tom Anderson was your first friend.

**486.** The majority of people pronounce the word "gif" with a hard G.

**487.** Sunkern is often in polls found to be the most disliked Pokémon character.

**488.** Capybara teeth never stop growing.

**489.** On May 12, 1937, King Edward VIII's coronation was supposed to happen, but he abdicated, so his brother, King George VI, was crowned instead.

**490.**   1978 was the most recent year that saw three popes; Paul VI, John Paul I, and John Paul II.

**491.**   1881 was one of 2 years that saw three presidents of the U.S.; Rutherford Hayes, James Garfield, and Chester Arthur.

**492.**   2022 was one of 2 years that saw three prime ministers of the United Kingdom; Boris Johnson, Liz Truss, and Rishi Sunak.

**493.**   Rutherford Hayes is the first U.S. president to use a telephone while in office.

**494.**   James Garfield knew and taught Latin and Greek; he also campaigned in 2 languages: English and German.

**495.**   Chester Arthur was known as a night-owl and didn't go to bed until 2 or 3 in the morning.

**496.**   The most popular hobby in the UK in 2024 was reading.

**497.**   According to a 2023 study, only around 15% of people are "self-aware".

**498.**   William Harbutt, a teacher from Bath, England, invented plasticine in 1897.

**499.**   The microwave oven was invented as a result of an accidental discovery of the heating power of microwaves for cooking.

**500.**   The number 500 in binary is 111110100.

**501.** Greece always leads the Olympic Games opening ceremony because it is where the games originated. Each country follows Greece in alphabetical order, based on the host nation's language, and the host nation comes last.

**502.** During the 2004 Olympics in Athens, Greece, the above rule did not apply. The host country, Greece, was introduced last and St. Lucia went first because it was first alphabetically.

**503.** Christmas Day is the most popular day to propose.

**504.** The least popular day of the week to get married is Tuesday.

**505.** "AKB48" in 2010 was recognised as the largest music group with 48 members, they have since risen to 130 members.

**506.** Alex Day's single "Forever Yours" reached No. 4 in the UK charts and was the first unsigned artist to reach the Top 5.

**507.** More than half of all energy used to produce electricity is wasted.

**508.** Alfred Hitchcock handcuffed Robert Donat and Madeleine Carroll together before filming a scene in the 1935 film "The 39 Steps." He pretended to have lost the key in order to put them in the right mindset for the scene.

**509.** Eisoptrophobia is the fear of mirrors.

**510.** The Fitzpatrick Scale is used to classify human skin colour for responses to ultraviolet light.

**511.** Banks first started introducing interest rates in the 3rd millennium BC.

**512.** The word 'mortgage' is derived from a French legal term meaning "death pledge".

**513.** In Denmark, it's considered rude to ask a person you've just met what they do for a living.

**514.** In 2020, Mexico was considered to have the worst work-life balance.

**515.** In the same study, the United Kingdom was 14$^{th}$.

**516.** "I am free of all prejudices. I hate everyone equally." is a quote attributed to W.C. Fields.

**517.** "A man who loves whiskey and hates kids can't be all that bad." is another quote attributed to W.C. Fields.

**518.** Marjorie Courtenay-Latimer, a 32-year-old museum employee from South Africa, rediscovered the coelacanth in the 1930s.

**519.** Knights in medieval times could avoid fighting in wars by paying a tax called 'scutage,' which was nicknamed a cowardice tax.

**520.** There is a difference between glue and adhesive. Glues are made from natural sources whereas adhesives are made from synthetic chemicals.

**521.** Measuring all adults as of 2022, 13 African countries have a higher literacy rate than the U.S.

**522.** A person with the blood type O- can donate to anyone.

**523.** A person with the blood type AB+ can receive blood from anyone.

**524.** Syncope is the scientific name for fainting or passing out.

**525.** The fastest production car in the world in the year 1990, was the Ruf CTR.

**526.** According to scientific research, people who wear mirrored sunglasses are more attractive.

**527.** In 2022, China was the world's largest exporter of padlocks.

**528.** The world's largest exporter of Christmas Trees is Denmark.

**529.** The gas mark is a temperature scale used on British ovens and cookers. The gas mark starts at 1 when the temperature is 275 degrees Fahrenheit. For every increase of 25 degrees Fahrenheit, the gas mark increases by 1.

**530.** Jeff Bezos originally wanted to call Amazon "Cadabra" until his lawyer pointed out that it sounded like cadaver.

**531.** The Bisexual Pride Flag was designed in 1998 by Michael Page.

**532.** Argon, a noble gas, gets its name from the Greek word "Argos," which means idle or lazy. This is because Argon is an inert gas.

**533.** In the TV series, Family Guy, the family dog Brian Griffin is a white Labrador retriever.

**534.** The word "turquoise" comes from the French word "turquois," which means "Turkish." This is because the gemstone was initially brought to Europe through Turkey.

**535.** The first country to ban all types and uses of asbestos was Iceland in 1983.

**536.** According to popular polls from Reddit & Strawpoll, the most popular Mortal Kombat character is Sub-Zero.

**537.** The book cover of the first book in this series was designed by Owais Ashraf.

**538.** Harry Kane's birthday is on July 28th, 1993.

**539.** The Bristlecone Pine tree, found in the western United States, lives the longest out of all known organisms, for over 5,000 years.

**540.** A giraffe named Forest, who is 12 years old and lives in Australia, has been verified as the tallest giraffe in the world, measuring 5.7 meters.

**541.** The word "veto" comes from the Latin meaning "I forbid".

**542.** The hat of a court jester is called a "cockscomb".

**543.** Roman General Mark Antony gifted the island of Cyprus to Queen Cleopatra of Egypt.

**544.** British Telecom printed their final phone books in March 2024.

**545.** The biggest users of glitter are unknown, but some common suggestions include the cosmetics industry, the military, boat painting companies, and the food industry.

**546.** In 2022, the world's largest exporter of handguns was Austria.

**547.** James A. Bonsack is credited as the inventor of the cigarette.

**548.** Fleas have 6 legs.

**549.** No species of flea is currently endangered or threatened.

**550.** Hamburgers have multiple invention claims ranging between 1885 and 1904 but are named after the port of Hamburg in Germany.

**551.** Lionel Sternberger is credited with inventing the cheeseburger. He did this in 1924 by simply placing a slice of American cheese onto a hamburger.

**552.** There are nine female names listed in Lou Bega's "Mambo No. 5".

**553.** Of all the women mentioned in the song who have birth data between 1999 and 2023, Jessica would statistically be the youngest.

**554.** Russia has won all the gold medals in artistic swimming from the Sydney Olympics in 2000 until the Paris Olympics in 2024.

**555.** Costco cashiers get paid more than Target cashiers in New York City as of 2024.

**556.** From the Sydney Olympics in 2000 until the Tokyo Olympics in 2021, only 11 American athletes have been disqualified.

**557.** Jamaica won its first Olympic medal in 1948.

**558.** On June 11, 2002, The House of Representatives of the U.S. officially acknowledged Antonio Meucci for his groundbreaking contributions to the development and invention of the telephone.

**559.** 10 days later, the Canadian government passed a bill recognising Alexander Graham Bell as the inventor of the telephone.

**560.** The first postage stamp to show the middle finger was released in Ukraine. It depicted a soldier flipping off a Russian warship.

**561.** Owls are more sensitive to light than humans.

**562.** According to Danish tradition, if you happen to be single on your 25th birthday, your friends will drag you into the street and cover you from head to toe in cinnamon.

**563.** Chevon is a culinary name for goat meat.

**564.** Daylight Savings Time was first introduced into Australia in 1917.

**565.** As of July 2024, there are 262 cubic kilometres of proven oil reserves remaining, which is a little over 46 times the volume of Lake Superior.

**566.** Lake Biwa is the largest freshwater lake in Japan.

**567.** Basketball and Volleyball were invented within 5 years and 20 kilometres of each other.

**568.** The Red Data Book of the Russian Federation is a document that lists rare and endangered plant and animal species.

**569.** In Northern Ireland, the letter 'H' is pronounced differently depending on whether you are Protestant or Catholic. Protestants pronounce it as "aitch" and Catholics pronounce it as "haitch". This pronunciation difference is known as a "Shibboleth".

**570.** In 1995, John Steele, who was 55 years old, gave Tracy Dolton, who was 24 years old, a lottery ticket as a tip. He promised to split the winnings if they won. They ended up winning $184,700 USD, so Dolton received $92,350 USD. This was the largest tip ever given at the time.

**571.** A Ranker poll from July 2024 showed that the most serious but hardest global problem to solve was war, followed by poverty in 2nd place and water pollution in 3rd place.

**572.** In July 2024, a Ranker poll revealed the Top 10 Disney princesses in descending order: Belle, Rapunzel, Mulan, Moana, Jasmine, Tiana, Ariel, Anna, Elsa, and Pocahontas.

**573.** According to another Ranker poll in July 2024, the best movie character of all time is Batman.

**574.** The first usage of the word "meme" was first documented by Richard Dawkins in 1976.

**575.** The first known use of the verb "yeet" according to the Oxford English Dictionary is from 1440.

**576.** Phyllis Galembo is an American photographer who earned an MFA from the University of Wisconsin in 1977.

**577.** In the 1881 census of Great Britain, people were asked to include their "rank, profession, or occupation." Some unusual titles like "Turnip shepherd", "Fish-bender", "Grape-dryer", "Knight of the Thimble", "Colourist of artificial fish", and "Proprietor of midgets" were documented.

**578.** The Indri (or the Babakoto) is the largest living lemur, weighing as much as 9.5kg and measuring up to 72cm from nose to tail.

**579.** In 2018, the primary agricultural export of Madagascar, with 4 million tons, was rice.

**580.** In 2022, Madagascar was the world's 18th largest exporter of rice.

**581.**   The first names of Frank Zappa's children are Moon, Dweezil, Ahmet, and Diva.

**582.**   On the 28$^{th}$ April 2004, an international friendly football match took place in Belfast between Northern Ireland and Serbia & Montenegro, the result was a 1-1 draw.

**583.**   The American Council on Education code states that tassels on mortarboards should be black or the colour appropriate to the subject to which there is an official list of subjects and colours (for example, Purple for Law and Pink for Music); however, gold tassels are reserved for those who have completed a doctorate.

**584.**   The "bowl of Hygieia" is a symbol most well-known in pharmacology.

**585.** "Hamas" was an Irish racehorse born in 1989.

**586.** Marcel Theroux, the brother of Louis, wrote a novel entitled "Strange Bodies" which won the 2014 John W. Campbell Memorial Award.

**587.** A person who was born in India from 26 January 1950 until 1 July 1987 is a citizen by birth, regardless of the parents' nationality; this rule was ended due to mass migration from Bangladesh.

**588.** The Russian state TV channel RT (Russia Today) is banned in the UK and several other countries.

**589.** Final Fantasy XVI and The Last of Us Part II are video games banned in Saudi Arabia due to homosexual related content.

**590.** A study published in a medical journal found that people who eat with their hands are slower eaters.

**591.** Blowing your nose at the table in Japan is considered impolite.

**592.** Fingers are never perfectly straight, as the finger bones are straight on the back side, but curved on the palm side.

**593.** The Joe Rogan Experience was the UK's most listened to podcast in 2023.

**594.** The most expensive mouthguard was worn by KSI, it had 108 diamonds and 24 carat gold leaf and was valued at over £40,000 ($51,328 USD).

**595.** There are 39 books in the Old Testament and 27 in the New Testament of the Holy Bible.

**596.** According to many surveys of readers of the Holy Bible, the most popular book of the Bible is the gospel of John.

**597.** As of 1$^{st}$ January 2024, the minimum wage in mainland Portugal for full-time workers is 760 euros per month.

**598.** There is no minimum wage in Somalia, South Sudan, and Sweden.

**599.** In the UK, the first alcoholic product to be advertised was Babycham in 1957.

**600.** Snakes smell with their tongue.

**601.** Pigeons, flamingos, and emperor penguins are the only birds that produce milk to feed their young.

**602.** Flamingo milk is red.

**603.** As of 2017, the song "Happy Birthday to You" is in the public domain.

**604.** Earth is the only planet not named after a god.

**605.** The average time that people wake up in the Netherlands is 7:47am.

**606.** Researchers have discovered that it takes 7 minutes for the average person to fall asleep.

**607.** In 1977, a police officer in Hawaii was awarded $39,000 USD who was struck by a falling coconut.

**608.** 1 person on average is killed by a shark every year in the U.S.

**609.** 2 people on average are killed by vending machines every year in the U.S.

**610.** The current speed record on water belongs to the late Ken Warby who reached 317.58mph (511.09kph) in 1978.

**611.** According to a 2018 study, only 3.3% of straight men would date a transgender person.

**612.** A kookaburra can fly up to 20 miles per hour.

**613.** You produce up to 10 litres of sweat daily.

**614.** A 2009 study reported that cows produce more milk when they are given names.

**615.** In 2002, Bruce Willis shipped 12,000 boxes of Girl Scout Cookies to U.S. soldiers in Afghanistan.

**616.** In 2013, a man in Los Angeles was arrested at a police sponsored gun buyback when he tried to return a pipe bomb.

**617.** Cheap Chic Weddings is a company that holds an annual Toilet Paper Wedding Dress Contest, the top prize in 2016 was $10,000 USD.

**618.** Processed cheese or American cheese was actually invented in Switzerland.

**619.** The first chimpanzee sent into space was named "Ham".

**620.** Ham the Flat Frog is an 11-inch plush sold by Fluffnest, retailing for $23 USD in July 2024.

**621.** The name of the man from the Quaker Oats brand, is Larry.

**622.** In 1567, the man with the world's longest beard, Hans Steininger; died from tripping over it when running away from a fire.

**623.** The coat of arms of Denmark has 3 lions.

**624.** The coat of arms of Sweden has 2 lions.

**625.** The coat of arms of Norway has 1 lion.

**626.** A peeled orange will sink in water, but an unpeeled orange will float.

**627.** Amaan Ramazan was a TV show in Pakistan. The show became controversial because it involved giving abandoned babies to parents who wanted them.

**628.** The city of Detroit awarded honorary citizenship to Saddam Hussein in 1980.

**629.** On average, it takes just under 5,000 lemons for a fatal vitamin C overdose.

**630.** The lifespan of a housefly is around 28 days.

**631.** In the UK, more people wear glasses or contact lenses than those who don't.

**632.** There are 8,760 hours in a year.

**633.** There are twice as many McDonald's restaurants than hospitals in the U.S.

**634.** There are 25% more McDonald's restaurants than hospitals in the UK.

**635.** The very first Drive-Thru restaurant in Europe opened in 1985 at the Nutgrove Shopping Centre in Dublin, Ireland.

**636.** The 3 most visited cities in Canada are Toronto, Vancouver, and Montréal.

**637.** The highest known concentration of vitamin C is the Kakadu plum.

**638.** Despite never leaving England, William Shakespeare set around one third of his plays in Italy.

**639.** Tally marks are different depending on where you are in the world.

**640.** The ivory figurine known as "Venus of Hohle Fels" is the oldest known depiction of a human being.

**641.** The most common reason why people visit doctors is for skin conditions.

**642.** The current world record for juggling 9 balls was set in 2006 by Anthony Gatto where he successfully juggled 9 balls for 55 seconds.

**643.** The creator of the PlayStation controller said that the circle and cross buttons represent the Japanese symbols for "yes" and "no". The triangle symbolizes a point of view and the square symbolizes a sheet of paper used to access menus.

**644.** There were 4,218 official titles released on the Sony PlayStation 2.

**645.** The average strawberry has 200 seeds.

**646.** The average apple has 10 seeds.

**647.** Babies blink less than adults.

**648.** You cannot breathe and swallow at the same time.

**649.** Around 2,300 species of bacteria can be found in your belly button.

**650.** The eye is considered to be the cleanest part of your body because of its ability to clean itself.

**651.** Matsumoto Hoji was an 18th century Japanese painter most well-known for his depiction of frogs.

**652.** The average human will consume 65 million calories in their lifetime.

**653.** According to a 2013 survey, the least popular car colour in Australia was brown.

**654.** The slide whistle dates back to at least the 1840s.

**655.** The average human burns around 11 calories per hour by chewing gum.

**656.** There are 135 steps on the Spanish Steps in Rome, Italy.

**657.** You can't sneeze while you're in REM sleep.

**658.** The song "Shiny Happy People" by R.E.M was the theme song for the unaired pilot episode of Friends, but it was later replaced by "I'll Be There For You" by the Rembrandts.

**659.** "LD 350-1" is a 2.8 million-year-old specimen widely regarded as the earliest recorded human.

**660.** "Marching on Together" is the motto of Leeds United Football Club.

**661.** The only 3-letter word that looks the same in lower-case when written upside-down is "pod".

**662.**   Bullerby syndrome refers to positive stereotypes about Sweden, like wooden houses, midsummer, elk, forests, and happy people.

**663.**   In British English, the word "blonde" refers to the same hair colour. However, in some languages like French, "blond" is used for men and "blonde" is used for women to indicate the hair colour.

**664.**   As of August 2024, 8.6% of U.S. Presidents have been assassinated.

**665.**   Early models of U.S. typewriters only had 24 keys and the numbers 1 and 0 doubled up as the letters I and O respectively.

**666.**   666 is the sum of the squares of the first 7 prime numbers.

**667.**   A tongue-twister is a phrase or set of words that is difficult to pronounce quickly because of similar letters or sounds.

**668.**   A tongue-twister in sign language is called a "finger-fumbler".

**669.**   "Kho Kho" is a sport primarily played in India that has 15 players per team.

**670.**   The name of the Isle of Wight in Latin is "Vectis Insvla".

**671.**   American Airlines saved $40,000 per year on fuel costs by removing one olive from each in-flight salad.

**672.**   Many airlines choose to paint their aeroplanes white because white paint is the cheapest and thinnest, which helps save weight.

**673.** Dead Woman's Hole, Grey Dick Hill, Horse Knob, and Soily Bottom Point are the names of real places in New South Wales, Australia.

**674.** The world's largest fan measures 8.48 metres long and 5.18 metres high, created by a company called Goods of Desire.

**675.** The world's happiest city in 2024 was Aarhus, Denmark.

**676.** In 2024, the world's 7th happiest city was Bristol, United Kingdom.

**677.** The only letters that don't appear on the periodic table are J & Q.

**678.**   Joya Williams is a former Coca-Cola employee who in 2006 tried to sell Coca-Cola secrets to Pepsi. Pepsi responded by notifying Coca-Cola, eventually leading to her arrest.

**679.**   According to the U.S. Patent and Trademark office, the phrase "IT'S ON LIKE DONKEY KONG" was filed as a trademark in 2010, the trademark was cancelled in 2020.

**680.**   When you leave a party without saying goodbye and quickly exit, it can be called a "French exit," "Irish Goodbye," or "leaving like the English." The specific term used depends on your location.

**681.**   There are more Lego mini-figures than there are humans on earth right now.

**682.** The voice actors of SpongeBob SquarePants and Karen Plankton are married in real life.

**683.** Out of the Eon Productions James Bond 007 films, Rotten Tomatoes and Business Insider ranked "A View to a Kill" as the worst James Bond film.

**684.** The human eye is very sensitive. In a dark night, if the Earth were flat, a candle's flame could be visible from a distance of more than 50 kilometres.

**685.** In 2018, two-thirds of American millennials thought the earth was flat.

**686.** Not long after Edinburgh Park railway station was built in 2003, it was discovered that there were no toilets.

**687.** M10 9KC is the fictitious postcode for the UK soap opera, Coronation Street.

**688.** Coronation Street was originally known as "Florizel Street" until an assistant pointed out that it sounded like a brand of disinfectant.

**689.** Chickens have great memories & can recognize over 100 faces.

**690.** Humans are capable of making up to 10,000 facial expressions.

**691.** Lettuces and Sunflowers are members of the same family.

**692.** The world's most consumed edible oil is Palm oil.

**693.** Flossing your teeth can improve memory by preventing gum disease, which can lead to memory problems caused by stiff blood vessels.

**694.** The Ethiopian calendar consists of 13 months.

**695.** Bees do a dance called the waggle dance to tell other bees where to find food.

**696.** The largest species of amphibian native to the UK is the common toad.

**697.** 702 is an American R&B girl group formed in Las Vegas.

**698.** "Snout Thinners" is an anagram of "Stinson Hunter."

**699.** In Karate, the yellow belt marks the first significant advancement in learning. It symbolizes the first rays of sunlight on a student and is one rank higher than a white belt, which is given to beginners.

**700.** 43.3% of Germans agree with the statement "Most people can be trusted".

**701.** 74.1% of Danes agree with the statement "Most people can be trusted", this is the highest in Europe.

**702.** Only 2.8% of Albanians agree with the statement "Most people can be trusted", this is the lowest in Europe.

**703.** "Wipeout", "Puppetry", "Etiquette", and "Typewriter" are words that can be typed only by using keys from the top row of a QWERTY keyboard.

**704.** Fireman Sam's fire engine is called Jupiter.

**705.** Dandruff affects around 50% of the adult population worldwide.

**706.** Wee Hymen Smooth is an anagram of "Show Me The Money".

**707.** Since 2017, the IKEA soft toy shark "Blåhaj" has become a symbol of the transgender community.

**708.** "Sandmott" is a brand of cushion sold in IKEA that retails for £5.00 as of August 2024 ($6.34 USD).

**709.** IKEA got its name from the founder's initials (I.K.), the farm he grew up on (E), and his hometown (A).

**710.** Tourists in Rome, Italy throw around €3,000 EUR in the Trevi Fountain every day.

711. There are around 350 different types of pasta.

712. According to a survey of Italians, the most popular pasta is penne.

713. The most used emoji in 2024 was the "face with tears of joy".

714. As of April 2024, the price to use the toilet in the McDonald's in Wenceslas Square, Prague, Czech Republic was 15 Czech Korunas.

715. The world's longest wooden escalators are based in the Tyne cyclist & pedestrian tunnels underneath the River Tyne.

716. JOR 1HO is a postcode serving Morin-Heights in Quebec, Canada.

717. Ontbijtkoek is a staple of a traditional Dutch breakfast: it's a rye cake spiced with cinnamon, nutmeg, ginger, and cloves.

**718.** In the Netherlands alone, 14 million kilos of Hagelslag are consumed annually.

**719.** King Henry V of England invented the first passport to help his subjects prove their identity in foreign lands.

**720.** "I'll show you that it won't shoot." were the last words of Johnny Ace who died aged 25 in 1954.

**721.** "Just be yourself, Sarah" were the last words of Queen Elizabeth II who died aged 96 in 2022.

**722.** A Boston cream pie is a cake with a cream filling. The dessert got its name when cakes and pies were baked in the same pans, and the words were used interchangeably.

**723.** The Oxford English Dictionary included a fake word "esquivalience" meaning the wilful avoidance of one's official duty; derived from the French word 'esquiver'.

**724.** A word that was added to the Merriam-Webster dictionary by mistake was "dord", the correct entry was supposed to be "d or d" as an abbreviation for density.

**725.** The Toyota Corolla is the world's bestselling car with Toyota building over 50 million of them since 1966.

**726.** Irv Gordon holds the record for most miles driven in a single car; his 1966 Volvo P1800S as of 2024 clocked an enormous 3,250,257 miles.

**727.** During the filming of Matilda, Danny Devito and Rhea Perlman, who played Matilda's parents, supported Mara Wilson by including her in outings with their family while she coped with her mother's battle and eventual death from cancer.

**728.** Matthew Broderick is left-handed.

**729.** The line in the capital letter Q is called a tail.

**730.** The line in the lower case letter q is called a descender.

**731.** There is a popular urban legend that claims William Shakespeare invented the letter Q. However, this is not supported by any evidence, as the Egyptians and Phoenicians had already used the same mark thousands of years before.

**732.**  The Roman numeral Q is sometimes used to denote 500,000.

**733.**  "Catch a cold", "uncomfortable", "break the ice", and "manager" were all words and phrases coined by William Shakespeare.

**734.**  600 squared is 360,000.

**735.**  In electronics, a "jiffy" is one-fiftieth or one-sixtieth of a second in most mains power supplies.

**736.**  The record low temperature in the month of June in Dubrovnik, Croatia is 10.0 degrees centigrade (50.0 degrees Fahrenheit).

**737.**  Chichester, England, is twinned with Ravenna, Italy.

**738.**  32nd U.S. President Franklin Delano Roosevelt has a film credit.

**739.** As of the 1ˢᵗ May 2024, the NHS prescription charge in England was £9.90 per item.

**740.** The planet Felucia in Star Wars was also known as Galush prior to the formation of the Galactic Republic.

**741.** In Star Wars, Darth Vader is 6' 8" or 203 centimetres tall.

**742.** The Boeing 747 was first introduced by Pan Am in 1970, and including the prototype, a total of 1,574 units were built.

**743.** York Haven Ltd. Is the only remaining company in the UK that produces carbon paper.

**744.** When measuring the intensity of earthquakes, the Richter Scale is mostly effective for regional earthquakes no greater than M5. The Moment Magnitude Scale is more effective for large earthquakes.

**745.** There are an estimated 100 earthquakes annually that measure M6 on the Moment Magnitude Scale.

**746.** A newborn baby's body will contain only around a cup of blood.

**747.** The Man with the Golden Gun is the James Bond film with the fewest kills, with Roger Moore's character only killing one person.

**748.** Any Catholic may perform an emergency baptism, such as if a person is in grave danger of death. The validity of the emergency baptism depends on the wishes of the person and if they consent to the baptism.

**749.** JRD Tata is considered the father of Indian civil aviation. In 1929, he became the first person to get a commercial pilot licence in India, with 'No. 1' on his licence.

**750.** Steve Jobs, the ex-CEO of Apple, was a vegan and had an interest in Zen Buddhism. He even considered becoming a monk in Japan.

**751.** The first screenplay is thought to be from Georges Méliès and his 1902 film 'A Trip to the Moon'. The film is silent, but the screenplay still contains specific descriptions and action lines that resemble a modern-day script.

**752.** Eja Lange born on 12th August 2001, is the son of Shania Twain.

**753.** Photographers say "say cheese" to make people smile for a photo.

**754.** In Bulgaria, photographers would make people say "зеле" meaning cabbage to get the same result.

**755.** Jacob Christoph Rad invented the sugar cube in 1841.

**756.** Although it's highly unlikely, diseases can be transmissible by farting.

**757.**   Luxembourg Airport was formerly known as Findel Airport.

**758.**   FC Differdange 03 were the winners of Luxembourg's top football division in 2023-24.

**759.**   The oldest ever Olympic athlete was Oscar Swahn of Sweden, he was 72 years and 281 days old when he competed in the 1920 Olympic Games.

**760.**   Joël Robuchon was a chef with the most Michelin stars awarded; he held 31 stars.

**761.**   According to a 2013 study, a mother will be pregnant for approximately 268 days.

**762.** The film 'Clue' based on the board game was released on December 13, 1985. Each cinema received one of the three endings, and some showings announced which ending the viewer would see.

**763.** The board game Cluedo is known as Clue in North America, the name is a portmanteau of 'clue' and 'ludo'.

**764.** Huzaifa Matovu of Uganda is widely regarded as the world's best Ludo player, winning the 2022 World Ludo championship.

**765.** Walter "Taffy" Holden was an engineer in the Royal Air Force with limited flying experience. In 1966, he accidentally flew a fighter aircraft when he engaged the afterburner by mistake. He was airborne for 12 minutes.

**766.** In 1818, Abraham Thornton was accused of murdering Mary Ashford. He asked for a trial by combat, which was a legal option at that time. However, his accuser declined the challenge. As a result, Thornton was acquitted.

**767.** In 2002, Leon Humphreys from Bury St. Edmunds was in court over a minor motoring offence that carried a £25 fine. He asked for trial by combat, claiming it was allowed under European Human Rights laws. However, the court disagreed and fined him £300.

**768.** Around 65.8 billion chickens were consumed as meat in 2016.

**769.** A study from 2023 revealed that people with ADHD are almost 3 times more likely to develop dementia.

**770.** On May 1, 1943, Staff Sergeant Maynard "Snuffy" Smith put out a fire on his aircraft by urinating on it. He was later awarded the Medal of Honor for this action.

**771.** In Christianity and Islam, Adam is considered the first person. In Hindu beliefs, the first person is Manu, the forefather of humanity.

**772.** Eating around 20-30 cherry pits is usually enough to induce cyanide poisoning.

**773.** Phosphoric acid has the chemical formula $H_3PO_4$.

**774.** An average of seven cases of the plague are reported each year in the U.S.

**775.** The largest crater on the near side of the Moon is the Bailly crater.

**776.** A camel typically drinks a litre of water per second.

**777.** There are no mosquitoes in Iceland.

**778.** Marlon Brando was the first actor to earn a million dollars for a single film, 1962's Mutiny on the Bounty.

**779.** The first actress to make a million dollars for one film was Elizabeth Taylor in the 1963 film Cleopatra.

**780.** Set-jetting, also known as location vacations, is the trend of travelling to places where movies and TV shows were filmed.

**781.** The principal ingredients of vinegar are acetic acid and water.

**782.** The average surface speed of the water at the head of the Mississippi River is about 1.2 miles per hour.

**783.** Condylostylus is a genus of flies and is thought to have the fastest reflex response in the animal kingdom. Scientists have measured its reflex response time to be less than 5 milliseconds.

**784.** Studies suggest that a small percentage of adults, around 1 to 2 percent, experience bed-wetting. However, it is believed that this statistic is not accurate due to the embarrassment associated with the issue.

**785.** Bees and wasps usually don't bother humans unless they are provoked. A risk analysis from Harvard claimed that your chance of being stung by a bee is 6 million to 1.

**786.** On average, around 100 people die annually from chewing on a pen.

**787.** The only country in the world without any churches is Saudi Arabia.

**788.** Royal Mail will allow you to send live bees in the postal system.

**789.** Royal Mail does not allow you to send frozen water in the postal system.

**790.** In 1903, Horatio Nelson Jackson and Sewall Crocker became the first people to drive an automobile across the U.S. Starting in San Francisco and finishing in Vermont. The vehicle used for the trip is now displayed in the National Museum of American History in Washington, D.C.

**791.** Luxembourg has the highest external debt per person. As of May 2024, the country's external debt amounts to 3.79 trillion USD, which equates to 5.79 million USD per person.

**792.** Aux is not a valid word in Scrabble but Aah is.

**793.** The average gym membership in Australia costs $70 AUD per month.

**794.** In 2020, the five most popular baby names for girls in Portugal, in descending order, were: Maria, Leonor, Matilde, Carolina, and Alice.

**795.** In 2020, the five most popular baby names for boys in Portugal, in descending order, were: Francisco, João, Afonso, Tomás, and Duarte.

**796.** 801 and 385 are the area codes for phone numbers in Salt Lake City, Utah.

**797.** The average bite force of a human is between 120 and 160 PSI.

**798.** The most featured cheat code in video games history is the Konami Code. It first appeared in the NES game Gradius in 1986 and has been used in 151 games so far. The code is Up, Up, Down, Down, Left, Right, Left, Right, B, A.

**799.** Pakkirappa Hunagundi from India suffers from a rare eating disorder and is addicted to eating bricks, gravel and mud.

**800.** Vanadium has the atomic number 23.

**801.** The world's largest strawberry structure measures 14.5 metres tall and is based in Strawberry Point, Iowa.

**802.** Nyctophobia is the fear of the night or of darkness.

**803.** In 2017, the average book had a length of 273 pages.

**804.** Grossular Garnets are gemstones that come in almost every colour, except blue.

**805.** The modern 23$^{rd}$ wedding anniversary gift is a silver plate.

**806.** The modern 13$^{th}$ wedding anniversary gift is furs or textiles.

**807.** Old Moore's Almanack is an astrological almanac that offers predictions and has been published in Britain since 1697.

**808.** Don't confuse the former publication with Old Moore's Almanac, which has been published in Ireland since 1764. This book has made successful predictions, including an assassination attempt on Donald Trump in 2024.

**809.** The capital city of South Sudan is Juba.

**810.** "The drive of your life" was an advertising slogan used by Peugeot.

**811.** An ell is a measurement equivalent to 45 inches.

**812.** The Benetton fashion brand was founded in Italy by Luciano, Carlo, Gilberto, and Giuliana Benetton.

**813.** A pentadecagon or pentakaidecagon is a name given to a polygon with 15 sides.

**814.** In 2010, a Swiss driver received the biggest speeding fine ever when he was caught going 57kph (35mph) over the speed limit in his Ferrari Testarossa. His fine was €137,000.

**815.** If you earn £500 per week, it would take you just over 38 years to have earned £1,000,000.

**816.** "Cry Havoc and let slip the dogs of war" is a phrase spoken by Mark Antony in Act 3, Scene 1 of William Shakespeare's Julius Caesar.

**817.** Fredric Baur, the inventor of the Pringles can, has some of his ashes in a Pringles can.

**818.** Nobody knows who invented the fire hydrant because the original patent was destroyed in a fire.

**819.** 'The Tribute to Doha' is a door handle encrusted with diamond dust and gemstones and backlit using an LED system. It is priced at around €100,000 making it the most expensive door handle in the world.

**820.** Most shark species have never been observed mating in the wild.

**821.** The United Kingdom, Australia, New Zealand, and South Africa usually spell it as 'yoghurt,' while the United States prefers 'yogurt'.

**822.** Yoghurt is a probiotic so if you put yoghurt inside a dead person, it will speed up the decomposition process.

**823.** There are 9 yellow specks in the logo of UK supermarket chain, Morrisons.

**824.** Adult cats only meow to humans, not to other cats.

**825.** The 'Chopard De Rigo Vision' is the most expensive pair of glasses in the world. It is made of 60 grams of pure gold and has several stones. Its price is $400,000 USD.

**826.** The most expensive property in the French version of Monopoly is "Rue de la Paix".

**827.** The four train stations in the British Monopoly game are "Kings Cross Station", "Marylebone Station", "Fenchurch Street Station", and "Liverpool Street Station".

**828.** The American version of Monopoly has four stations: "Reading Railroad," "Pennsylvania Railroad," "B & O Railroad," and "Short Line Railroad".

**829.** A male ballet dancer is called a 'ballerino'.

**830.** A staple of most workplace team-building exercises, the tallest spaghetti and marshmallow tower measured 65 inches (165 centimetres) tall.

**831.** Norbert Pozsonyi and Aliz Totivan set a world record by building a spaghetti bridge that held 443.58 kg.

**832.** "Mezzanine" scores 79 points in Scrabble.

**833.** A maisonette has a front door that opens directly outside the home and the living space is split over two floors, like a house. Flats, on the other hand, are on just one floor, with each room on the same level.

**834.** As of 2021, the country with the most patents per million people is South Korea.

**835.** Bob Switzer invented the high visibility jacket in 1933 after getting injured while unloading crates at a Heinz Ketchup factory in California.

**836.** Bulbo By Campana Brothers is a chair resembling a nest that is sold by Louis Vuitton for £70,500 ($89,940 USD).

**837.** The colour orange was named after the fruit of the same name.

**838.** Known in the Caribbean as a pomerac, the Otaheite apple is a pear-shaped fruit with red skin and white flesh.

**839.** The rarest Xbox achievement is called Day One. It was released at the launch of the Xbox One and was available to fans who purchased the Day One Edition of the console.

**840.** The hotter a fart is, the faster it spreads.

**841.** Ants do not have lungs.

**842.** The programming language Python is named after Monty Python.

**843.** Your brain gets lighter as you get older.

**844.** Researchers found out that it takes 1,000 licks to finish a lollipop.

**845.** The first product invented by Sony was a rice cooker.

**846.** Ngerulmud, the capital city of Palau, is the least populous capital city of a sovereign state.

**847.** Amber Heard, Meghan Markle and James Corden have all been voted the most disliked celebrities of 2024.

**848.** The Thalamus is part of the brain.

**849.** A plumassier is a professional that deals with ornamental feathers.

**850.** Frances Bissell is a food writer.

**851.** A partly broken fracture is also known as a 'greenstick' fracture.

**852.** Carlisle stands on the banks of the River Eden.

**853.** The shortest possible air distance between London and Beijing is 5,059 miles (8,142 kilometres).

**854.** Freddie Mercury, the lead singer of Queen, was born in Zanzibar and attended school in the Indian city of Mumbai.

**855.** 8 to the power of 8 is 16,777,216.

**856.** During the Gulf War, Operation Desert Sabre lasted for approximately 100 hours.

**857.** Pity Me is a place found in County Durham, England.

**858.** Susurrant is another word for whispering.

**859.** Miliaria is a condition more commonly known as prickly heat.

**860.** Adolf Hitler's favourite dish was Leberklösse (liver dumplings). He was also very fond of sweets, including chocolate, buttered scones, and Führer Cake.

**861.** Führer Cake, named after Hitler, was an apple cake coated and sprinkled with nuts and raisins that had to be baked and left for Hitler daily.

**862.** Chanakhi is a Georgian stew made with lamb, aubergines, potatoes, tomatoes, and herbs. It is said to be Joseph Stalin's favourite dish.

**863.** Titan, the largest moon of Saturn, is mostly Nitrogen.

**864.** There were 204 newborns in the U.S. with the given name Jupiter.

**865.** Contrary to popular belief, the modern alcoholic spirit Amaretto is made from apricot kernels, not almonds.

**866.** Wired Magazine in 2020 proclaimed that the video games console with the most iconic startup is the Sony PlayStation.

**867.** Tafari Makonnen is the birth name of Ethiopian Emperor Haile Selassie.

**868.** On Christmas Day, the 25th of December, King William I of England was crowned, and Mikhail Gorbachev resigned as leader of the Soviet Union.

**869.** There is a species of fungi named after SpongeBob SquarePants; it's called "Spongiforma Squarepantsii".

**870.** Solder is the alloy of lead and tin.

**871.** Allodoxaphobia is the fear of other people's opinions.

**872.** The Eiffel Tower can grow up to 15 cm taller in the summer because the iron expands when it gets hot.

**873.** If a sound is mellifluous, it's a sound that is pleasingly smooth and musical to hear.

**874.** Teeth are the only part of the body that cannot heal themselves.

**875.** The Ancient Romans used to drop a piece of toast into their wine for good health, hence why we 'raise a toast'.

**876.** Venus is the only planet in our solar system to spin clockwise.

**877.** In high concentrations, nutmeg is hallucinogenic.

**878.** A chef's hat is known as toque, it traditionally has 100 pleats and is meant to represent the supposed 100 ways you can cook an egg.

**879.** In 2014, there was a Tinder match in Antarctica.

**880.** The flag of Missouri has the most stars of any other U.S. state with a total of 61 stars.

**881.** M&Ms are named after Forrest Mars and Bruce Murrie, the businessmen who created them.

**882.** The Chupa Chups logo was designed in 1969 by the surrealist artist Salvador Dalí.

**883.** Humans are the only animals that blush.

**884.** All the clocks in the 1994 film Pulp Fiction are set to 4:20.

**885.** The high school sets in iCarly, That's so Raven, and Saved By The Bell are the same.

**886.** The blob of toothpaste on a toothbrush is called a 'nurdle'.

**887.** Candles used to be made of beef fat or bees wax, and as a result they were eaten during famines.

**888.** Because his body will belong to the Roman Catholic Church, the pope cannot be an organ donor.

**889.** When he was assassinated, Julius Caesar was stabbed 23 times.

**890.** Nepal has the most public holidays of anywhere in the world, with 39.

**891.** James Cameron sold The Terminator script to Gale Anne Hurd for $1.

**892.** Finland has more saunas than cars.

**893.** In the 2000s, the Royal Mail spent £1 million on red rubber bands that were used to tie bundles of letters at sorting offices. Many complaints were received about the number of bands littering the streets.

**894.** There are no moles in Ireland.

**895.** The draft copy of this book has more memory than the computer that took Apollo 11 to the moon.

**896.**   Park and Ride is a service that provides parking lots and bus transportation to help people avoid parking in the city centre. The first example launched in the UK was in Oxford in the 1960s.

**897.**   The first zebra crossing was introduced on Slough High Street, England on 31 October 1951.

**898.**   Christopher Columbus rationed pickles to his sailors to keep them from getting scurvy.

**899.**   As of 11th August 2024, Rick Astley's "Never Gonna Give You Up" amassed 1,562,240,741 views on YouTube.

**900.**   Eritrea, Hungary, Myanmar, Tajikistan, and the U.S. are the only countries that tax its citizens regardless of their residency.

**901.** Ó Caiside is a Gaelic surname; it's more well-known and anglicised as "Cassidy".

**902.** There are around 200 piano tuners in New York City.

**903.** Portugal discovered and colonized the uninhabited São Tomé and Príncipe islands in 1470.

**904.** Joe Snape and Will Jarvis broke the record for the longest recorded hug, they hugged for 36 hours, 36 minutes, and 36 seconds in June 2018.

**905.** According to the USDA, 100 grams of custard has 122 calories.

**906.** Venezuela has the cheapest petrol in the world, costing only 2p per litre thanks to government subsidies.

**907.** A sloe is a small fruit also known as a blackthorn.

**908.**   A halberd is a medieval weapon consisting of an axe blade and spike.

**909.**   5 stone equals 70 pounds in Imperial measurement.

**910.**   Former British Prime Minister Tony Blair supports Newcastle United football club.

**911.**   In the TV series "King of the Hill", Hank and Peggy's surname is Hill.

**912.**   Colette Besson is an Olympic 400m champion.

**913.**   The average person blinks around 20,000 times per day.

**914.**   4040 divided by 20 is 202.

**915.**   A strong sign that you're in love is that your significant other's heartbeat will sync with yours.

**916.** Lemon trees can produce up to 600 pounds of lemons in a year and can grow up to 20 feet tall.

**917.** A tangelo is a hybrid between a tangerine and a grapefruit.

**918.** According to a 2023 survey, the most hated food is the anchovy.

**919.** All humans have been born on earth.

**920.** All of the clock hands meet when the time is 09:49:05.

**921.** The English towns of Sutton Coldfield, Tunbridge Wells, Leamington Spa, and Wootton Bassett all have the prefix Royal.

**922.** "Perfect 10" by The Beautiful South is a song that includes innuendos about body image, focusing on dress sizes and penis sizes.

**923.** In a 2000 poll, "The Birdie Song" was voted the most annoying song of all time.

**924.** Pope Benedict VIII died on the 9th April 1024.

**925.** Hannah and Lauren Luckey have the longest snapchat streak in the world, 3,400 days and counting as of August 2024.

**926.** In 10 minutes, a hurricane releases more energy than all the world's nuclear weapons combined.

**927.** Sliced bread was invented on July 8, 1928.

**928.** In Spanish culture, the tooth fairy is a mouse.

**929.** Tornadoes spin anti-clockwise in the Northern Hemisphere and clockwise in the Southern Hemisphere.

**930.**　McDonald's is the largest distributor of toys in the world.

**931.**　The average lifespan of a Lithium Ion battery is 2 to 5 years.

**932.**　In 1980, a Las Vegas hospital fired some workers for betting on when patients would die.

**933.**　It's illegal for minors to play pinball in South Carolina.

**934.**　With 7 million students, the Indira Gandhi National Open University is the largest university in the world by student population.

**935.**　The largest university in the UK by student population is the Open University with 205,000 students.

**936.**　A 2002 Renault Clio hatchback retailed for £9,290 when new.

**937.** It takes around a week for your eyes to adjust to a new pair of glasses.

**938.** The average reader can read between 200 and 300 words per minute.

**939.** In the U.S., Domino's Pizza delivers over one million pizzas every day.

**940.** According to a 2024 study, around 20% of married men cheat on their spouses.

**941.** The average age of a Ferrari owner is 51.

**942.** The average age of a Bentley owner is 45.

**943.** A British gymnast survived a fall from a hotel window by performing a somersault and landing on his feet.

**944.** Strawberries are the only fruit with seeds on the outside.

**945.** A Croque Monsieur is a toasted ham and cheese sandwich with the bread dipped into beaten egg before it's cooked.

**946.** A Croque Madame is the same as a Croque monsieur but with a poached or fried egg on the top.

**947.** Chia seeds come from the desert plant Salvia hispanica, a member of the mint family.

**948.** Ducks quack differently depending on the region they are from.

**949.** As of midnight on the 12th August 2024, it was 27 degrees centigrade (81 degrees Fahrenheit) in Agadir, Morocco.

**950.** The original website for the 1996 film Space Jam is still online as of 2024.

**951.** Humans shed around 3.6kg of dead skin each year.

**952.** According to research in 2017 and 2024, most people prefer to eat ice cream from a cup rather than a cone.

**953.** Wiping off sweat doesn't actually help your body cool down.

**954.** The oldest language in the world that's still spoken is Tamil.

**955.** Berlin has more parks and green spaces than any other city in Europe.

**956.** In the U.S., it's illegal to own a 1933 Double Eagle $20 coin.

**957.** The world record for the longest flight ever took place in 1958 in a Cessna 172 that flew nonstop for 64 days, 22 hours, and 19 minutes and covered 150,000 miles (240,000 kilometers).

**958.** The Pride of America is the only U.S. flagged cruise ship.

**959.** The country with the most registered ships is Panama.

**960.** Nam Co is a lake in Tibet.

**961.** Namco was an entertainment and video game company founded in 1955.

**962.** A licence to run a hot dog stand in New York City can cost up to $400,000 USD a year.

**963.** Skill testing questions are a legal requirement attached to many contests and lotteries in Canada.

**964.** 11 babies have been born in Antarctica.

**965.** Antarctica has the lowest infant mortality rate at 0%.

**966.** The most common colour used in tattoos is black.

**967.** Cruise ships have a morgue on board.

**968.** Friends of Dorothy is a slang term for gatherings for members of the LGBT+ community, referencing the main character of The Wizard of Oz.

**969.** Pyongyang is not in the scrabble dictionary, but if it were it would score 19 points.

**970.** A dog's nose print is as unique as a human fingerprint.

**971.** Dogs have three eyelids.

**972.** In 2018, Budgy smugglers were voted as the most disliked clothing item in the UK.

**973.** The closest point between Ireland and Great Britain is 12.5 miles (20 kilometres) apart.

**974.** Blackjack is the most widely played casino game in the world.

**975.** A goldfish will eventually turn pale if left in a dark room.

**976.** The collective noun for foxes is a skulk.

**977.** The most common prescribed item in the U.S. in 2022, was Atorvastatin.

**978.** Microsoft Word was invented in 1983.

**979.** Ariana Grande is allergic to bananas.

**980.** Asteroid 52665 is named in honour of Queen guitarist Brian May.

**981.** Eucrasite is an anagram of Cauterise.

**982.** According to the Bank of England inflation calculator, £1 in 1524 is worth £833.15 in 2024.

**983.** 'View of Delft' is an oil painting by Johannes Vermeer.

**984.** In Irish tradition, the seventh son or daughter are thought to have been bestowed with special powers.

**985.** A native or resident of Sydney, Australia is called a "Sydneysider".

**986.** Larissa is the 4th largest moon of Neptune.

**987.** In heraldry, addorsed means back to back.

**988.** The fall in pitch of a vehicle's siren as it passes is an example of the Doppler effect.

**989.** The gestation period of a sheep is around 152 days.

**990.** Research suggests that black vehicles are involved in accidents much more frequently than cars of any other colour.

**991.** The average delay for a Japanese Shinkansen train is around 20 seconds.

**992.** Thomas Jefferson is said to have brought the first waffle iron to America in 1789.

**993.** Playwright Tennessee Williams briefly worked as a caretaker on a chicken farm.

**994.** Tomatoes are the most consumed vegetable in the world.

**995.**   In 2000, Fusaichi Pegasus became the most expensive horse ever sold, for $70 million USD.

**996.**   The film "For Your Eyes Only" was filmed on the Greek island of Corfu, and the Mareblue Hotel on the island has wings named after James Bond characters.

**997.**   Cuba has the most physicians per person out of any country, with around 8.4 doctors per 1,000 people.

**998.**   In 1965, Brian Robson mailed himself in a wooden crate from Melbourne, Australia in a desperate bid to return home to the UK; he was intercepted by officials in Los Angeles where he recovered in hospital before he was deported. He published a book of his experience called "The Crate Escape" in 2021.

**999.** The standard size for a UK letterbox is 254 mm x 38 mm.

**1000.** The human tongue has 8 muscles.

# Outro

Hey! So, this has nothing to do with that awesome M83 song, but it's still a perfect track. By the way, guess what? I published a new book with random facts! Super proud of it, gotta say. It's like this insane compilation of facts, the biggest one ever put together, you know? And get this, I'm thinking of attempting a Guinness World Record for reciting the most facts in an hour! It's a record that hasn't been officially tried before, but I've got a ton of knowledge already gathered. Pretty cool, huh?

I want to thank all the companies and individuals who have taken the time to share their knowledge on forums, books, magazines, and the Internet, no matter how relevant it is to certain subjects.

I'm done with useless information for the moment. I will most likely be taking a break from writing books for at least 2 years so consider this as my parting gift for a short while. I need to pause writing for a while to focus on getting my bus licence and moving to a new house. I want to apply for a degree because I've been delaying it for 2 years and want to go back to some form of education.

Writing down goals or promises increases the likelihood of following through with them. However, only time will determine if I have indeed kept these promises.

I expect to receive messages notifying me about errors or outdated information. I welcome such feedback, and I am willing to make the necessary changes.

However, when it comes to new information, I currently have more pressing matters to attend to. Although there are new projects in progress, my focus is currently on more important tasks. To quote the late, great David Bowie: "*I don't know where I'm going from here, but I promise it won't be boring.*"